THE
WELL-TEMPERED
SENTENCE

A Punctuation Handbook

THE WELL-TEMPERED SENTENCE

*for the Innocent,
the Eager, and the Doomed*

KAREN ELIZABETH GORDON

Ticknor & Fields
New Haven and New York •

Designed by Christine Swirnoff/Libra Graphics, Inc.

Library of Congress Cataloging in Publication Data

Gordon, Karen Elizabeth.
The well-tempered sentence.
1. English language — Punctuation.   I. Title.
PE1450.G65   1983   421   82-19704
ISBN 0-89919-170-3

Printed in the United States of America
P 10 9 8 7 6 5 4 3

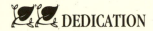# DEDICATION

I can't possibly give this book to one person, but certain sentences in it are for David Bromige, Judith Wright, Harold Schneider, Baillie Kay, Robert Bly, Carol Dunlop, and Kay Turney.

For their ineffable assistance, I wish to thank Linda Purdy and Maia Gregory. And thanks to Paul Aaen Gordon for his definition of Time.

CONTENTS

INTRODUCTION

Reader, I have finished with this little farrago which you are only now about to begin. I have lowered the final periods and parentheses into place, have dusted and resharpened my claws. What is a comma but a claw rending the sheet, the asthmatic's gasp? What is a question mark but what's needed to complete this thought? Punctuation: what is it, after all, but another way of cutting up time, creating or negating relationships, telling words when to take a rest, when to get on with their relentless stories, when to catch their breath? (And you — you are breathing, are you not, in the same rhythm that creates words?)

We don't really know who invented the comma, but a typical Roman sentence couldn't make it with fewer than ten of these metrical incursions which are the tics of prose. The Egyptians had no use for commas (or periods, semicolons, or question marks — and exclamation points were the exclusive domain of priests), but they scratched their ideas and drew them and were not too troubled with sound. Hieroglyphics, it is true, are coming back (see your TV screen or any bathroom wall if you doubt it), but words haven't died out of the language yet; and whether you like it or not, you've got to punctuate. Punctuation marks are a part of the vocabulary of civilization; a misunderstanding can be created or erased by them. Be brave: it is less difficult than you might suppose.

The door flies open and abruptly you are inside. The book is about to begin! A rapping sound, then scurrying and scuffling noises come from within. An indiscreet guffaw is heard from a room far away. A verandah rattles, a water pipe shudders, and a drawer is heard to slam. Somewhere a petticoat is being smoothed down. There are so many characters to compose themselves, to freeze mid-sentence, as it were, the sentences each of them is caught in. For if nothing else, this book is staggering with inhabitants, crammed with protagonists. And so many of the characters remain unnamed, pronouns whose mysterious antecedents appear to be lurking elsewhere, as if you have blundered into a story already started. And these *are* stories, in their small totalities; there is no want of drama here! Someone has obviously been the houseguest of Rosie and Nimrod, but who was it that misbehaved? Might there be some relationship between the cold bathwater and the stale beer that you're not privy to, some connection other than that expressed by the commas in an insinuating list? Are Rosie and Nimrod married, or are they living in sin?

Loona, pacing hypnotically through some cloak-and-dagger or existential histrionics, is quite aware of the state of waiting she is in, but does she know what for? The tiptoe pose tilting toward some unseen horizon cannot be held for long without stressing her hidden tibia. An out-of-doors setting can be conjectured for her impatience, or a very drafty chamber anyway, to account for the wind-blown quality of her beauty — or is this mere dishevelment? Have her toes turned blue with her lips in this frozen vigilance? She has not yet succumbed to despair: there's too much rapture in her face.

What word follows "darling" during that spelling lesson whose master reveals his hyphenated passion to a nameless, ageless child? Or is she Charlotte Tingle, the sophomore whose acquaintance we have already made?

These and other questions must either remain unanswered or be further explored by you, the reader. Oh, I am so eager to entrap you in these pages, these words and situations where I too have been, I can barely speak!

THE
WELL-TEMPERED
SENTENCE

THE 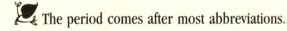 PERIOD _____

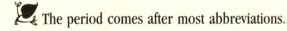 The period is used to mark the end of a declarative or mild imperative sentence.

> The room filled up with philanderers, all seeking some buxom relief.

> Take your hands off me.

> Stay a while.

> Don't get jittery on me.

> You don't have to give me all the gory details about how you got hepatitis.

> Let us settle our indifferences.

> I have just begun to explore the possibilities of the next disaster.

 The period comes after most abbreviations.

> Ms.

> MS.

> M.S.

A period comes after numerals or letters in a vertical list.

1. camels	a. Herzegovina
2. dromedaries	b. Abyssinia

Do not use a period at the end of a sentence that is part of another sentence.

> The rage and irony in his voice (I could hardly fail to notice the scorn with which he addressed me) alternated with a solicitous smile.

> Le Beau's remonstrance, "You are always late and unwelcome besides," made her apologize and cry.

Periods belong inside parentheses or brackets enclosing an independent sentence. If the enclosure is part of a larger sentence, the period is placed outside the parentheses or brackets. Periods go within quotation marks except when single quotation marks set off special terms.

> They were curled up beside their radio listening to Gustav Mahler's "I'm Gonna Lock My Heart."

> We were hard at work on the second revision when Samuel slapped my face. (He had shown such irrational devotion to his own opinions before.)

Pouring her peignoir over her bored shoulders, she harumphed, "My God, what a somnolent suite of nocturnes that was" (and what a very voluptuous drowsiness is to follow, she added to herself as she pressed his dressing gown upon him and feigned a languorous yawn).

She said, "I have just finished writing 'The Treacherous Bend in the Rainbow.'"

THE QUESTION MARK

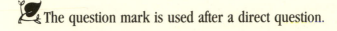

The question mark is used after a direct question.

Where have you been that's interesting enough to send you home like this?

Who's taking the money at the door? And how shall I dress to not seem real?

Warum sprach Zarathustra?

What's on your schedule to ruin today?

Taking up the slack in your tongue?

Why did I look *rhapsodize* up in the phone book?

Who's the big cheese around here?

How can I get in your way when you don't even have one?

 The question mark expresses editorial uncertainty.

Saint Fracas (456?–458 A.D.) had a short but raucous childhood.

 A request or order surreptitiously or politely phrased as a question does not end in a question mark.

Will you pardon my shabby get-up and ravish me again.

Would you please muffle your little commotion and straighten out your mugs.

A question mark can turn a declarative or imperative sentence into an interrogative one.

You don't mind playing croquet in the mud?

You call that disgusting display of suburban vernacular a bon mot?

You're not mad?

A question mark does not come after an indirect question.

Odious flogged our flagging spirits after asking whether we would object.

Only when the question mark is part of quoted or parenthetical material does it go inside the quotation marks, parentheses, or brackets.

Do you agree with Proust that "each of us finds lucidity only in those ideas which are in the same state of confusion as his own"?

The last time I'd seen him (how long *had* it been?) he was a fugitive in a sea-blue bus.

A question mark should stay at the end of an interrogative sentence that is part of another sentence.

How had this dreadful suspicion arisen? was everyone's question in that tense saloon.

We were still pondering the eternal question, Was the Big Bang an act of passion or the Freudian slip of an arrogant fool?, when the storms and floods began.

In Spanish, an inverted question mark comes before the interrogatory sentence and an upright one comes after it.

¿Qué tal, Pepe?

THE 🦋 EXCLAMATION POINT

🦋 The exclamation point is used after an exclamatory word, phrase, or sentence and in some cases after an ironical comment.

> What a surprise to find you here alone!
>
> What governance lies in a well-versed tongue! What jeopardy for me!
>
> Ouch! That feels good!
>
> I mean, this is not the approving nod of a nincompoop!
>
> Oh, no! Not another one of your hairy friends!
>
> And don't you dare set foot in my hearse ever again!
>
> What a swell soirée this has turned out to be!
>
> You filthifier of English dreams!
>
> Was I ever crestfallen!
>
> How exciting to see you in traction again!

🦋 When it belongs to the quoted or parenthetical material in a sentence, an exclamation point goes inside the quotation marks, parentheses, or brackets.

> "You uxorious lummox!" the woman bellowed in response to his muffled pleas.

What a swell soirée this has turned out to be!

"I can hardly believe my eyes!" he ejaculated at the canyon's edge.

Then he stroked my nose (I tell you, he really does love me!), and he mumbled into my cleavage, and suddenly burst into tears.

In Spanish, the exclamation point comes before the sentence, inverted, as well as after it, right end up.

¡Qué playa hermosa!

THE 🖋 COMMA

🖋 The comma is used between independent clauses of equal value that are short and have no commas within them.

> He shot pool, he drank Anchor Steam beer, and he rarely went home.

🖋 A comma comes between two independent clauses joined by coordinating or correlative conjunctions, such as *and, but, or, nor, neither, yet, for,* or *so.*

> I haven't done it yet, so I don't think I could do it again.
>
> I begged to differ with him, but he refused to see me that way.
>
> You have no idea how happy I am, and furthermore I'm not about to give you one.
>
> The suspect removed his grimy white gloves, but another pair lurked beneath.
>
> Either I've been missing something, or nothing has been going on.
>
> You crossed my mind, but you didn't stay there.
>
> I'm too young to remember, and you're too old to forget.
>
> We sat around waiting for some epiphany, but only a

foghorn broke through the silence and encroached on the monotony of our crouching figures.

It was one of those cases of no news being good news, and that was not nearly good enough.

🍃 A comma is needed after a dependent clause, usually a fairly long one, that precedes an independent clause.

When it became apparent that they were just pulling our legs, we started kicking.

As far as I'm concerned, all phone calls are obscene.

🍃 Two or more verbs having the same subject (a compound predicate) are not to be separated by commas.

She woke up and gave the world a hurt look.

Rosamund counted her lymph nodes and then returned to the tabulation of her toes.

His words skidded across the living-room floor and landed in her lap.

My dermatologist said I should eat lots of skin but did not specify whose.

She unfurled her umbrella in the dark and muttered obscenities into its awful folds.

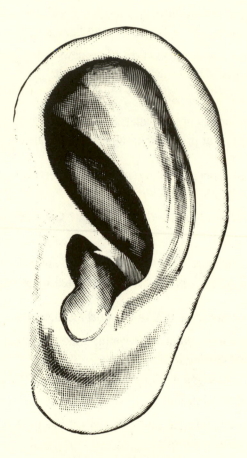

As far as I'm concerned,
all phone calls are obscene.

He pressed her fragrant fingertips to his lips and remorselessly told her the hideous truth.

She always carries bandages with her but will give them only to bleeding people to whom she has been formally introduced.

Her bejewelled puissance quivered across the foyer and set the ushers to quaking in their boots.

Use commas to set off the one or ones spoken to in direct address.

Come here, Nicolas, and hold my mouth shut with your big, spring-loaded hands.

Friends, you needn't have come all this way just to have a tiff.

Appositives—words that follow a noun or pronoun and identify it—are usually set off by commas if they are nonrestrictive. Such words add parenthetical information.

Nobiscus Kahn, professor of Angst, used to cry all over his lectern and ruin his lovingly prepared notes.

Charlotte Tingle, a sophomore, was the only girl at the lodge that night.

27

Her cat, Mount Diablo Base Line as Seen from Highway 395 Just North of Bridgeport, knew how to give an admirable back rub with his well-tempered and discreet claws.

He lay dreaming of her little smile, a miracle of frailty and avarice.

If the appositive is restrictive, commas are omitted.

The poet Wallace Stevens was a pedestrian too.

James Joyce's novel *Ulysses* was once an article of coveted and contraband smut.

A comma is used between two adjectives when they modify the same noun and the word *and* could be used between them without altering the meaning.

We entered a large, disreputable museum.

Justinian said farewell once more to the sad, sad faces of his donkeys.

He wanted to eat her peachy, creamy complexion with his souvenir spoon from Yellowstone Park.

She let out a low, false chortle.

She greeted him with open, entrenching arms.

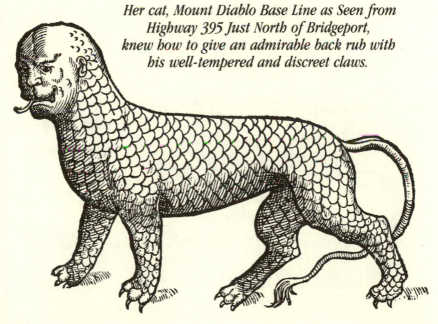

Her cat, Mount Diablo Base Line as Seen from
Highway 395 Just North of Bridgeport,
knew how to give an admirable back rub with
his well-tempered and discreet claws.

*In these laconic gestures,
she conveyed the story of the creation,
the history of the world,
and a prognosis for the ensuing millennium.*

Time is a slippery, viscid, wavering tool of a malignant prestidigitator with nineteen thumbs.

🌿 If the first adjective modifies the idea set forth by the second adjective and the noun combined, no comma is used between the adjectives.

She lay tastefully dying in an unruffled green gown and never once complained.

Her dull gold eyelids lifted heavily and fluttered one final coquettish farewell.

🌿 An adverbial phrase beginning a sentence is often followed by a comma.

From the right, the moon rises like a proud tangerine.

Before stepping out, Charmiane locked the last remaining secret drawer.

Because of this baffling situation, we all gave up and adjourned to a nearby bar.

After he painted her face and knees, they sauntered out into the lugubrious crowd.

In these laconic gestures, she conveyed the story of the creation, the history of the world, and a prognosis for the ensuing millennium.

A comma comes before and after an adverbial phrase or clause occurring in the middle of a sentence between the subject and the verb.

> The little orchestra, before treating us to an evening of scabrous melodies, stuffed themselves with snails.
>
> Georgia, after lifting her petticoats, turned the corner in her clattering heels.
>
> Mitzi, in a manner that surprised everyone present, broke into a hefty aria and then proceeded to swallow a sword.

The comma is sometimes not used after short introductory adverbial phrases.

> At dawn the sun began to rise.
>
> At breakfast we consumed a reprehensible buffet of assorted Nordic things.
>
> In utero her son-to-be sulked.

A comma is not used after an introductory adverbial phrase immediately preceding the verb it modifies.

> Out of the bushes appeared a well-dressed man with his head underneath his arm.

In the hallway danced a bevy of folk-struck maidens with flowers and snakes in their hair.

Out of this domestic chaos emerged a placid and resolute truce.

A restrictive dependent clause (a clause that would alter the meaning of the main clause if omitted) that follows a main clause should not be set off by a comma. A nonrestrictive clause in the same position is preceded by a comma.

I will accompany you to the spa if we can go hear Ornette Coleman afterwards.

He agreed to this arrangement, although he doesn't really like jazz.

Commas set off nonrestrictive phrases and nonrestrictive clauses giving descriptive information not essential to the meaning of the sentence.

The engineer, who was asleep at the time, missed the apparition floating past the windows of the train.

Raymond, who usually wears overalls, showed up in a green kimono.

The final act of the play, which was unevenly hilarious, took place on a drifting barge.

*If your intentions
are really good,
I'll never
understand them.*

After a day's hike through torrid regions of my own body, I arrived at a small oasis manned by a carry-over of an old lover, who awaited me with cool drinks and a million flies.

No comma is used with a restrictive, or essential, clause.

The guys who are bald are made to sit on the south side of the room.

Other fortresses under his jurisdiction have never sought clemency for March hares.

Anyone who disagrees with me had better step forward and explain his recalcitrance at once.

All laughter that is out of place will be stuffed into a nearby drawer.

A dependent clause coming before the main clause should usually be set off by a comma whether it is restrictive or not.

Should you die, I'd go mad so I could talk to you all the time.

If you'll take me where I want to go, I'll take you where you think we are.

If snow is wet, what is light?

If your intentions are really good, I'll never understand them.

An introductory participial or infinitive phrase should be set off by a comma unless it immediately precedes, and forms part of, the verb.

Entering the room, she found herself generously ignored.

Skimming along the water was a cement truck full of mice.

Menacingly bopping down the road, the thug consulted his horoscope and decided to take the day off.

Ululating through her tears and yanking her tresses, the young widow paused to take a deep breath and admire herself in the mirror.

Stuffing her mouth with tarts, the duchess announced that she was leaving the country at the side of a worthless lout.

Aghast at this revelation, the duke backed into the fire and seriously singed his nether parts.

Ominously snuffling into her sleeve, the duchess departed into the black and inveigling night.

To get the rest of it off your chest, you would have to remove your shirt.

To remove the smudge from her record, she sorely effaced herself.

🌿 A comma sets off absolute phrases (phrases composed of a noun or pronoun plus a participle that are not joined to the rest of the sentence by relationship words).

Her hands being cold, she plunged them into her inadequate pockets and tried to appreciate the snowstorm as an elemental treat.

Her hair matted with greasepaint and her magnificent torso protruding from a negligee of green nylon, she maundered through the apartment house next to her own thrusting her key into each astounded door.

🌿 A comma should set off a parenthetical clause, phrase, or word that is logically close to the rest of the sentence. Parenthetical elements less logically related to the rest of the sentence should be set off instead by dashes or parentheses.

The disconsolate child picked up the rubber remnants of his glorious red balloon and felt, in the flabby skin of such pathos, a darkness in the depths of his rubber soul.

37

His last girlfriend, it was believed, had never stood him up or put him down.

Those spurs are, I must say, a provocative addition to your wardrobe.

Kristin Langfeldt — a regular bluestocking she was — couldn't find a viable tunnel for her art.

The concert ended with a sonata (by then I was fast asleep) by Beethoven, Schumann, or Liszt.

A comma follows the exclamatory *oh* but not the vocative *O*.

Oh, how ridiculous!

O gentle king!

Oh, regrettable night!

Use commas to set off interjections, however mild, transitional adverbs, and other expressions that cause a break in the flow of thought.

Well, she feels like some phenomenon, but she's really just a shaken belief.

What is love, after all, but a cross between two wishes.

Well, this is a pleasant exhaustion.

Yes,
I would like another one
and in a different glass.

Indeed, the storm damage was worse than we had feared and greater than our enemies had wished.

Come, please, and bring your brother's wife.

Sorry, we don't deal in ultimatums.

Yes, I would like another one and in a different glass.

Dear me, how you have sacrificed your ethereal beauty for a life of greed and smut.

Why, whatever are you doing with that towel?

When such expressions don't break the continuity and no pause is needed, commas are unnecessary.

We are perhaps rather tedious company after some of the places you've been.

I do in fact prefer raucous company but am delighted to be here nevertheless.

We did therefore have a pleasant evening of staring numbly amongst ourselves.

Two or more complementary or antithetical phrases referring to a single word following them should be set off from one another and from the following words by commas.

His delicate, though at the same time rough, cheek

brushed against her sleeve and ripped it to silken shreds.

The most desired, if not the least convenient, seat in the house was taken by a dummy in diamonds and furs.

Your conclusions lead me away from, rather than toward, what you want me to think.

 An antithetical phrase or clause starting with *not* should be set off by commas if it is unessential to the meaning of the modified element.

He is a man of the world, not the punk you take him for.

The women in the room, not the men, are the best judges of the sexism of that remark.

I came to you, not to hear your stories, but to bounce upon your knee.

 But —

I came to you not so much to hear your stories as to bounce upon your knee.

 Interdependent antithetical clauses should be set off by a comma.

I came to you not so much to hear your stories
as to bounce upon your knee.

The less she knew about the other woman, the more elaborate and tormenting her fantasies became.

Think what you wish, I'll never go dancing again.

The lower she sank, the better she felt.

🦃 Short antithetical phrases, though, don't require commas.

The sooner the better.

🦃 Three or more elements in a series are separated by commas. When the last two elements (words, phrases, or clauses) in a series are joined by a conjunction, a comma comes before the conjunction.

Across her pellucid and guileless complexion danced a motley choir of alibis, innuendoes, disguises, and sobriquets.

He looked at her face, her thighs, her hands for some sign of approbation, but everything about her was glancing away, in the direction of something he could not name or escape.

We gave ourselves over to an interregnum of discord, mockery, and delight.

The rest of the story can be figured out by gossip, slander, and false report.

The oleaginous hors d'oeuvres were followed by beakers of vodka, remorse, and cold soup.

He is walking up walls, crawling sideways, and turning somersaults as he approaches the queen.

She is paranoid, quite correct, or seeing too much as she considers this matter.

He, she, and it all agreed on their common name at once.

The turgid prose of the wedding ceremony gave way at the gala reception to biting remarks, caustic hors d'oeuvres, and drunken apologies, which the newlyweds fled in a rented BMW for a little spa frequented by clerics and crooks.

🌿 When elements in a series are very simple and are all joined by conjunctions, no commas are used.

The truth of her checking account was mysterious and awkward and sad.

He thought the remark she'd made was brilliant or irrelevant or mad.

She led a complicated and secret quotidian existence of matinees and intrigues and regrets.

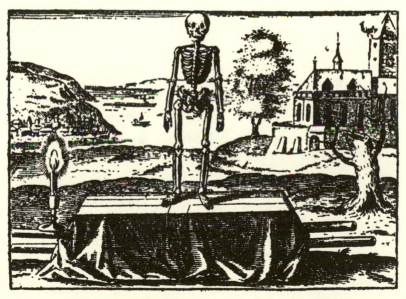

Think what you wish, I'll never go dancing again.

When a series is concluded with *etc.* in the middle of a sentence, the *etc.* is set off by commas.

> He told her he was into shuffleboard, soap operas, Lawrence Welk, etc., before she managed to slip out the back door.

> She powdered her nose, her body, her alibis, etc., to meet his scrutiny intact.

A comma is used after terms such as *that is, i.e., e.g.,* and *namely* when they are used to introduce a series or an example.

> Some of our members, namely, Alice, Bambi, and Bruno, had better watch out what they are saying these days.

> I advise you to split, i.e., beat it, get out, if you know what's good for you and your howling family.

Sometimes a comma must appear to prevent mistaken junction.

> To Lila, Nemo was ever a forethought.

> To Nemo, Lila was barely an afterthought.

> He followed her career as it rose and flowered, and

applauded each new whiff of success she snorted on her distant but lonely laurels.

Shortly after, the convocation commenced its pompous tones and hollow notes.

Two identical words should be separated by a comma for easier reading.

They came in, in striped pants and spats.

Whatever happens, happens because it must.

Unrelated numbers are also separated by a comma.

In 1905, 763 mustaches were shaved off in one county in Massachusetts alone.

Although they are not necessary, commas may be used to set off a phrase indicating place of residence or origin directly after a person's name.

Suki Trousseau of Pumpkin Center entered the room with a mop.

On her knees for the final flourishes was Suki Trousseau, of Pumpkin Center.

She led a complicated and secret quotidian existence of matinees and intrigues and regrets.

However, with historical figures whose places of residence or origin have become part of their names, the comma should be omitted.

> Alexander of Macedonia
>
> Eleanor of Aquitaine
>
> Labia of Slavonia

Words identifying a person's title or position are set off from the person's name by commas.

> Simca Cosmos, past and present president of the Femmes for Fatality, attended the convention on mortality at the Hotel Artaud.
>
> Sola Crespusci, poetry critic for *Licking the Beast*, was deluged with complimentary copies of the most aberrant works.

Commas are used to separate the parts of addresses and names of geographical places or political divisions.

> Winslow Thundermum, Ph.D., Secretary, 18 Red Red Road, Akron, Ohio, answers all questions you might ask of the society.

He rode his bike from Eyebrow, Utah, to Chicago, Illinois, in thirteen perspiring summer days.

In dates, the comma between month and year is optional, but commas must set off the year whenever it immediately follows the day.

> I was born on March 17, 1947, on a cold bed of sand.
>
> On 31 October 1972 a gang of hoodlums disguised as mendicant children gained entrance to the doomed chateau.
>
> In January 1979 a host of angels was espied off the shores of Lake Tahoe in a pleasure boat emanating the black and blue notes of early jazz.

A comma is used to indicate omitted material readily understood from the context.

> The farmer takes a wife; the wife, a child; the child, a dog; the dog, another child; the other child, another dog; the other dog, a pet rabbit to chase.
>
> Joe took the hard road; Millie, the easy street.
>
> Tina has tonsillitis; Herman, herpes.

He rode his bike from Eyebrow,
Utah, to Chicago, Illinois, in thirteen
perspiring summer days.

🌿 A comma follows the complimentary close of letters.

> With all the sincerity I can muster,
>   Nelda M. Zippel

> Yours inevitably,
>   Savannah Swift

🌿 A comma comes between every third digit, counting from the right, in numbers of one thousand or over.

> 196,950,000 kilos

🌿 Commas separate inverted names, phrases, etc., as in a bibliography, index, or catalogue.

> Roisterdoister, Ralph

> Manuel, A Manual For

🌿 A comma comes after the salutation of a personal letter.

> Dear Rosie and Nimrod,
>   Thank you for the hospitality, the cold
>   bathwater, the stale beer, and everything.

> Dear Arthur,
>   You make me talk big in my sleep.

A comma is used to set off conjunctive adverbs, such as *however, moreover,* etc., and transitional adverbs.

> We hate your ideas; however, we will give them proper consideration.

A quotation, maxim, proverb, or similar expression should be set off from the rest of the sentence by commas.

> The old man sat with his daughter muttering, "Shall I part my hair behind? Do I dare to eat a peach?"

> "I've been wondering, Jasmine," said Jimmy shyly, "if you'd care to sit this tango out in my lap."

> As he usually did when entering a strange room or agreement, he thought fondly and desperately of his motto, Be cool, which never did him any good.

> He remembered too late that vehicular proverb, People who drive in glass autos shouldn't have bones.

If the quotation is the subject, predicate nominative, or restrictive appositive of the sentence, the comma should not be used.

> "Get out, and take your mucus with you" was hardly the sympathetic greeting the flu victim expected from his healthy friends.

"I wanna lick the syrup off your hotcakes" was her favorite line in a song by Merlo Hag.

🖎 A comma is not used with an indirect quote.

G. K. Chesterton says that coincidences are spiritual puns.

Sola Crespusci remarked to her cohorts that poetry is mostly vacant exercises done at majestic hours and resigned from her thankless job.

🖎 A comma should not be used to set off a quote that fits logically into the rest of the sentence.

Dr. Kirkengog defined teasing as "an excessive attention to something you'd just as soon not have noticed at all."

🖎 When a comma is called for at the end of material within quotation marks, parentheses, or brackets, it goes inside the quotation marks but outside the parentheses or brackets.

For Max Ernst, collage was "an exploration of the fortuitous encounter upon a non-suitable plane of two mutually distant realities," and that definition is still relevant today.

Sola Crespusci, defining photography as "light plus the impulse to see more than it can reveal," took to photographing slices of the unexpected in the sordid back alleys of chance.

She scrunched her shoulder up next to his (all the while thinking of Timofey), and the shadows obligingly obliterated what was wrong with his face.

We were not thunderstruck (not even stunned), and her disappointing announcement gave way to a game of cards.

THE ⚘ SEMICOLON _____

⚘ A semicolon is enlisted when a more significant break in continuity than that indicated by a comma is called for.

⚘ A semicolon is used in compound sentences between independent clauses not joined by connectives, particularly if they are extended or have commas within them.

> Oh, I often click my tongue; it's my only revenge.

> Sit down; I'll make us some coffee and some suspirations.

> Visions, on the one hand, devour my brain; hyenas, on the other, feed on yours.

> Problems in the mismanagement of human emotions are becoming increasingly noticeable; specialists in these areas have given way to shoulder-shrugging and wheezing when confronted with real instances.

⚘ A semicolon punctuates the elements in a series for which further division than that provided by commas is needed.

> The contestants for the breakfast-eating championship came from Lompoc, Rhode Island; Laundro, Green

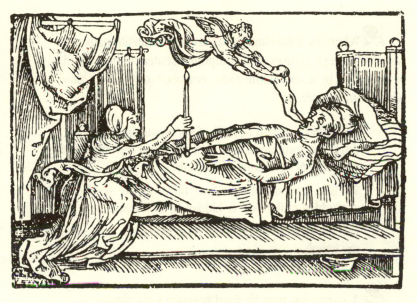

Sit down;
I'll make us some coffee
and some suspirations.

Hungary; Gravona, New Shropshire; and other places we'd never heard of.

When the following words are used transitionally as adverbs between clauses of a compound sentence, they should be preceded by a semicolon: *then, however, moreover, thus, hence, indeed, yet, so.*

> Samantha had had her fill of his blustering histrionics; thus, she spun around on her heel and retreated to the coolness of her dimly lit boudoir.
>
> We like the look of your face; however, we suspect that a troubled childhood is hidden by that beard.
>
> I've got you under my skin; moreover, you have invaded my lymph.

A semicolon may be used between long clauses of a compound sentence or ones subdivided by commas, even with a conjunction joining them.

> Jacob, who was sitting on the balcony watching her out of the corner of his steel-gray eye, lunged forward to touch her as she passed by; but someone grabbed a fistful of his collar from behind and said, "Lay off my woman, you jerk."

Not only were we naked, crazed, and starving
(and far from our warm little homes);
we were without any good books as well.

The semicolon goes outside quotation marks or parentheses. When quoted matter ends with a semicolon, the semicolon is dropped.

> Yolanta seemed to think that everyone in the world had read "Rameau's Nephew Meets Rappacini's Daughter"; she referred to it in every conversation she had.

> This was only one of the signs of her coming dementia (many more were yet to manifest themselves); her delusions became progressively more literary and bizarre.

> Not only were we naked, crazed, and starving (and far from our warm little homes); we were without any good books as well.

THE
COLON _____

The colon is used to stress the connection between two clauses that form a single sentence or to separate one clause from a second clause that illustrates or amplifies the first.

A colon is used to introduce a part of a sentence that exemplifies, restates, or explains the preceding part.

> Some of the world's great monsters have untold stories: many, in fact, led quite happy childhoods before their later, more infamous years.

> I've led a sheltered life: I've gone from one shelter to another.

> Pain stood in the way like a sheet of glass: you could walk through it, but not without a certain noise.

The colon is used to introduce a series or list.

> Coco concentrated her study on three twentieth-century French writers: Raymond Queneau, Blaise Cendrars, and Corolla Dewlap.

If the list or series comes after an expression such as *namely, for instance, for example,* or *that is,* a colon should

Some of the world's great monsters have untold stories:
many, in fact, led quite happy childhoods
before their later, more infamous years.

be used only if the series consists of one or more grammatically complete clauses.

Coco's study was concentrated on three twentieth-century French writers, namely, Queneau, Cendrars, and Dewlap.

For example: Queneau is the author of *The Bark Tree;*

Cendrars wrote *To the End of the World;* and Dewlap is a prose poet of sensuous renown.

🌿 The terms *as follows* and *the following* require a colon if followed immediately by the illustrating or listed items or if the introducing clause is incomplete without such items.

The way to her heart was as follows: take a left many times and then go straight.

The following people will be shipped a dozen yellow roses upon their respective demises: Chortle T. Ashbottom, Percy Q. Festivall, Dorothy Lambleton, and Nestor Craymom.

🌿 If the introducing statement is complete and is followed by complete sentences, a period may be used instead.

A guide to the churches follows. Each one is to be visited in its turn. The village is full of them.

1. Begin with the Church of the Wandering Magi. . . .

🌿 A colon is used to introduce an extended quotation.

The speaker rose and spoke as follows: "It wasn't always that people wore red shoes . . ."

🌿 A colon comes between the chapter and verse numbers in Biblical references.

Noah's long, wet story begins in Gen. 5:28.

🌿 A colon is used between the volume and page numbers in reference to large works or periodicals.

We got a run-down on bananas in the *Encyclops Laconnica* 2:147.

🌿 A colon may appear after the salutation of a business letter.

Dear Sir:

I wish to complain, without seeming to, for otherwise I am completely satisfied with all your errors, ineptitude, and faux pas.

🌿 A colon separates the hours from the minutes in expressions of time.

The man in the red cape followed me until 2:17, when he was seen stepping into the men's john for a change of clothes, a new profession, or a change of scene.

A drug: It gives you back all the headaches the world has stolen from you.

🍂 A colon is used to separate the parts of a ratio.

The suspended animation rate and the mortality rate for Sylvester County are in the ratio 7:51.

🍂 A colon may separate a heading from the material it describes or introduces.

An accomplished man: no trouble with strange fastenings.

Falling in love: I was acting in accord with my favorite hyperboles.

HELP WANTED: Retired, active couple to menace small mobile-home park.

Headline: STREET HUSTLERS EVADE SCHEHERAZADE

Sign on librarian's desk: REVENGE

A drug: It gives you back all the headaches the world has stolen from you.

A valentine: Oh, to be up against you.

Headline: TWO DECLARED DEAD IN TINY SOB

🍂 A colon separates the name of a character from his lines in a play.

LADY ZIPWORTH: All I do is wait for your clumsy hands to
make mincemeat of my apparel.

A colon can be used to separate the title and subtitle of
a book.

> *The Mourning of the Logicians: A History of the
> Decline of Reason in Western Civilization*
>
> *Om, Om on the Range: Cowboys and Meditation*
>
> *The Reverberating Rubber Band: Life as Seen through
> a Slingshot*

The colon should appear outside quotation marks or
parentheses. When material ending with a colon is quoted, the
colon is dropped.

> There was one thing that left her unsatisfied at the end
> of that novella *(The Telltale Toothbrush):* she never
> found out who the heroine really was.
>
> She winced at his response of such a gratuitous "Wow":
> it said little for his seizure of her meaning and even less
> for his lexicon.
>
> He had a strenuous objection to the poem "Suddenly
> What Sings in Me Dies of Boredom": it was a blatant
> piece of plagiary.

THE HYPHEN

A hyphen connects the parts of some compound words used as nouns or adjectives. It is also used in some words formed with prefixes.

> The starry-eyed sycophant prowled about the antechamber in her underwear, her catlike movements foreshadowing the self-conscious grace of her imminent and all-out attack.

> "That was a curiosity-provoking peepshow," said the pseudosophisticated ball-of-fire to the pink-faced stick-in-the-mud as they cuddled halfheartedly over a pint of bitter in a Neo-Gothic hole-in-the-wall.

> A well-known cross-eyed scholar-poet with gray blue eyes and coal black hair drove many an ill-favored maiden to madness with his devil-may-care attitude.

But a hyphen is not used when a compound adjective comes after the noun or when the first word is an adverb ending in -ly.

> The mannerism was well studied.

> Her neatly categorized notions of human frailty were summarily reviled.

The mannerism was well studied.

🌿 A hyphen shows syllabification — the break between syllables — at the end of a line.

> When she was depressed, and that was
> pretty often, she would pluck her eye-
> brows and drink Southern Comfort and
> sing the most disgusting songs.

> She was a splendid combi-
> nation of talent and trouble.

🌿 A hyphen joins compound numbers from twenty-one to ninety-nine and is used to express fractions.

> thirty-six
>
> eighty-seventh
>
> two-thirds

🌿 But the fraction should not be hyphenated if one element of it already has a hyphen.

> forty-four hundredths
>
> one sixty-fourth

🌿 When numbers are not spelled out, hyphens link them

with units of measurement to form adjectives. Money figures, however, are hyphenated only when spelled out.

> The 5,000-year-old fossil lay grinning in his palm.

> Their rendezvous at the Last Judgment Pinball Machine Motel turned into a 254-hour marathon that neither Torquil nor Jonquil would ever regret.

> A $5 million deficit may be something to snivel about, but it need not derange one's dreams.

 But —

> The waiter sniffed at his five-dollar tip and softly clucked his insouciant thanks.

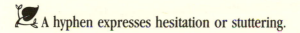 A hyphen expresses hesitation or stuttering.

> "I'm d-d-delighted to see you again," she stammered, barring his way into the room with her big toe spread out to its full size.

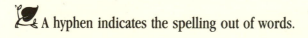 A hyphen indicates the spelling out of words.

> "You are my darling, my d-a-r-l-i-n-g," said the spelling master to his rapt and evasive pupil as he opened her eyes to a whole lexicon of shame.

THE DASH

The dash shows a break in continuity or thought in a sentence.

> Last night, as we slept together for the last time — where were you, anyway?

> I've had a lot of things on my mind lately — now what was I saying? — I mean, I can't concentrate, palpitate, ruminate; why are you looking at me that way?

The dash is used to emphasize an appositive.

> More than just a book — it's a major piece of torture.

> Theodora, my beloved — my only soporific — how sweet of you to tuck me into bed.

A dash sets off parenthetical material that results from a break in thought or continuity.

> She had goose pimples — or were they goose bumps? — all over her cool, luscious flesh.

> I cleaned my sealskin — and what a chore it was! — only to find that there were fifty more filthy ones beneath it waiting for the same treatment from me.

It was twilight — if ever there was a time to match that word — and the stars were beginning to rear their shiny heads. . . .

A dash is used before the citation of the author or source of a quotation, etc.

"Every dog has his hay to guard." — Trillenspiel

"Great men are not always idiots." — Grandpa

"It's a disgrace to the written world."
— *The Splenetic Review*

"A Sargasso of the unintelligible ineffable."
— Percy Fly-by-Night

"I hear as the stags in the underwood hear when they raise, point, and lower the great hairy auricles of their independent pink ears." — Henri Michaux

"Unrequited love's a bore." — Billie Holiday

A dash is used between numbers, dates, times, places, etc., that mark limits. In this case, however, a shorter dash appears. It is called an en dash because in set type it is the width of a capital *N*. (Type it as a hyphen.) The dashes previously discussed are em dashes and are as wide as a capital *M*.

You will find the secret of the lost Albanian on pages 89–111.

Gradimir the Timid lived 1439–1502.

The Lobelia Relocation Office is open 1:00–4:30 daily and would be glad to relocate your lobelias, or anything else you want misplaced.

He left on the Nismer–East Blagundia Express in haste and in the hope of having a good lunch.

MULTIPLE  PUNCTUATION _____

When two different punctuation marks express themselves at the same point in a sentence, the stronger of the two wins, and the other is dropped.

> "Haven't you had enough time perusing that menu?" cried the waitress, grinding her teeth and stamping her little ripple-soled feet.

> He was banging on the door and bellowing, "Open up, you adorable beast!"

QUOTATION MARKS

 Quotation marks enclose direct quotations and dialogue.

She said, "As a rule I hate iguanas, but this one had a wistful face."

I wish people wouldn't say "Excuse me" when I *want* them to step on my feet.

"That wallpaper there, for instance, harbors great myopic discoveries in the surface of its sheen," she adduced.

The tampon ad read: "First she was a woman — then she was a teenager."

Who was it who wrote, "Life is a stage attacked by an idiot"?

"What are tears, anyway," she sobbed in his arms, "but little refugees from the ocean?"

Quentin Crisp elucidated, "No one wants to get into his grave still feeling frisky."

"And you can still smile after all those broken bottles and all that bad press?" he asked.

"Are you a student?"
"No, I'm a visiting metaphysician."

"Are you getting married?"
"It's a tossup between probably and no."

I wish people wouldn't say "Excuse me" when I want them to step on my feet.

In dialogue a new paragraph indicates a change of speaker.

> She bore it as long as she could, for she could hardly believe her own eyes, and then she said:
> "What on earth are you doing?"
> "Cletterin' the dishes, Robert Poste's child."
> "But surely you could do it much more easily with a little mop? A nice little mop with a handle? Cousin Judith ought to get you one. Why don't you ask her? It would get the dishes cleaner, and it would be so much quicker, too."
> "I don't want a liddle mop wi' a handle. I've used a thorn twig these fifty years and more, and what was good enough then is good enough now. And I don't want to cletter the dishes more quickly, neither. It passes the time away, and takes me thoughts off my liddle wild bird."
> "But," suggested the cunning Flora, remembering the conversation which had roused her that morning at dawn, "if you had a little mop and could wash the dishes more quickly, you could have more time in the cowshed with the dumb beasts."
> —Stella Gibbons, *Cold Comfort Farm*

For passages of one hundred or more words, indent and single-space the quotation and do not enclose it in quotation marks.

Why am I writing this? I have no clear ideas, I do not even have ideas. There are tugs, impulses, blocks, and everything is looking for a form, then rhythm comes into play and I write within that rhythm, I write by it, moved by it and not by that thing they call thought and which turns out prose, literature, or what have you. First there is a confused situation, which can only be defined by words; I start out from this half-shadow and if what I mean (if what is *meant*) has sufficient strength, the *swing* begins at once, a rhythmic swaying that draws me to the surface, lights everything up, conjugates this confused material and the one who suffers it into a clear third somehow fateful level: sentence, paragraph, page, chapter, book. This swaying, this *swing,* in which confused material goes about taking shape, is for me the only certainty of its necessity, because no sooner does it stop than I understand that I no longer have anything to say. And it is also the only reward for my work: to feel that what I have written is like the back of a cat as it is being petted, with sparks and an arching in cadence. In that way by writing I go down into the volcano, I approach the Mothers, I connect with the Center — whatever it may be. Writing is sketching my mandala and at the same time going through it, inventing purification by purifying one's self; the task of a poor white shaman in nylon socks.

—Julio Cortázar, *Hopscotch*

79

Quoted poetry should be centered between the left and right margins and single-spaced, without quotation marks.

Back alone in the mud!
Sinking in this darkness,
The depth of my own body
Feels like fences
Torn from the soil
                        —Karen Gordon

on earth, this mouth's
daily bread, mud
that sticks lovingly
in the treads
of essential shoes.
                        —Stephen Kessler

Short quotations from poems may be written with the rest of the running text, with quotation marks enclosing them and with slashes between the lines.

> Harold Schneider's "The Inquisition" continues: "Tell me about the footsteps/That go thump in your nightgown/Voices in the wide drawer by/The bed . . ."

A quotation within a quotation is punctuated by single quotation marks.

"A babel broke out, in which Aunt Ada could dimly be discerned beating at everybody with the *Milk Producers' Weekly Bulletin and Cowkeepers' Guide,* and shrilly screaming: 'I saw it . . . I saw it! I shall go mad . . . I can't bear it . . . There have always been Starkadders at Cold Comfort. I saw something nasty in the woodshed . . . something nasty . . . nasty . . . nasty . . .' "

—Stella Gibbons, *Cold Comfort Farm*

" 'Yes, I'm labefying my crumpet with all these nigmenogs,' replies Theo volubly."

—Raymond Queneau, *The Bark Tree*

Quotation marks enclose the titles of short stories and poems, chapters, essays, articles, television and radio programs, and short musical compositions. Periods and commas go inside quotation marks even when they are not part of the title.

The cyclical nature of existence was revealed to her in half-hour snatches of "As the World Churns," a soap opera about biodegradable triangles and the proper uses of centrifugal force.

"We Had a Dustbowl Love" was number one on the Country and Western charts for three weeks, giving way, in the fourth week of April, to "Josie, Is It True That You've Grown Hotter Than Your Tears?"

She kept herself company through part of that insomniac night with a short story called "The Mauled Scribe."

The premier performance of "Vermeer Nocturne" included a maiden in the timpani section sloshing cream in a large pink pitcher and a delicately lighted window through which the conductor waved his baton.

We went to a performance of "Des Knaben Wunderhorn" conducted by a Chicago cop.

She kept herself company through part of that insomniac night with a short story called "The Mauled Scribe."

PARENTHESES 🗲

🗲 Parentheses are used to enclose loosely related comments or explanations.

> He's probably out there (in the waiting room) sitting in his own lap.

> We took a tortuous route (through small talk, double-entendres, a few drinks, and some polite evasions) to arrive at a state of intimacy where we pleasantly admired our bodies.

> On Thanksgiving she served to her elders little birds stuffed with Walt Whitman poems and accompanied by goosed forefathers, Plymouth rocks (actually gallstones), and kerosene.

> The neighbors, in this sylvan, sometime paradise, are clobbering each other, and her toothless face is starting to rend my shirt (very Gothic), so I think I'll go mail this at the post office and get back to those French tangles of sensuous words.

🗲 Parentheses go around numbers or letters listing items in a series that are part of a running text.

> Chapman thought that Karen Snow-Mariée's "The Wretch of Lugubria" suffered from (1) pretentiousness, (2) pessimism, and (3) an effulgence of narrators.

We took a tortuous route (through small talk, double-entendres, a few drinks, and some polite evasions) to arrive at a state of intimacy where we pleasantly admired our bodies.

85

We had finished our Irish coffee. (We had plenty of time, we thought, to get to the theater.) We wanted to prolong that moment past fulfillment, bedtime, and death.

A parenthetical sentence within another does not begin with a capital letter nor end in a period. A freestanding parenthetical sentence between two other sentences, though, requires parentheses, a capital letter, and a period.

> I took my time getting close to him (in an utter stupor, I spent half an hour dressing while he waited for me below) and even longer to tell him my name.

> We had finished our Irish coffee. (We had plenty of time, we thought, to get to the theater.) We wanted to prolong that moment past fulfillment, bedtime, and death.

LOONA [pacing hypnotically]: *How long,*
how long must I wait?

BRACKETS

Brackets are used to enclose editorial remarks or words inserted as explanation within a direct quotation.

> "At that time, she [Tarantula Gadfly] was merely stage-struck and madly in love with herself."

Brackets enclose the remark *sic* to indicate errors, often in spelling, in quoted material.

> Her epistolary torrent ended, "Regretabily [*sic*] yours, Morgana Fey."

Brackets are used to enclose stage directions.

> LOONA [*pacing hypnotically*]: How long,
> how long must I wait?

ELLIPSES 🌿

🌿 Ellipses come in threes and fours, and each collection of periods has its function in indicating omitted words.

🌿 Three dots stand for an omission within or at the beginning of a sentence.

> Her hairdo, which was a collection of bald spots and carefully placed, elaborately dyed tufts, had to be mowed, snipped, and dyed every other week.

🌿 The above sentence shortens to:

> Her hairdo . . . had to be mowed, snipped, and dyed every other week.

> ". . . and furthermore, I have no use for your dirty politics, your coy mannerisms, . . . your subhuman monologues, . . . and your touching foibles which have endeared you to your many followers."

> ". . . but this is just the beginning of a long-haul bibliography secretly being prepared for the silent majority who await word from the inner limits of reason where folly and vision collide."

In order to make more sense of the quoted material or to indicate what has been omitted, other punctuation may appear on either side of the three ellipsis dots.

Compare this passage from Gogol's *The Nose* to the abbreviated version below it.

> "I won't even listen to you! Do you really imagine that I'll allow a cut-off nose to remain in my place, you old crumb! All you do is strop your damn razor and when it comes to your duties, you're no good. You stupid, lousy, skirt-chasing skum! So you want me to get into trouble with the police for your sake? Is that it, you dirty mug? You're a stupid log, you know. Get it out of here. Do what you like with it, you hear me, but don't let me ever see it here again."

> "I won't even listen to you! Do you really imagine that I'll allow a cut-off nose to remain in my place . . . ! All you do is strop your damn razor and when it comes to your duties . . . So you want me to get into trouble with the police for your sake? . . . You're a stupid log, you know. . . . but don't let me ever see it here again."

Four dots (a period followed by three spaced dots) are used to show omission of the final words of the quoted sentence, the first words of the following one, an entire sentence or more, or a complete paragraph or more. A question mark or exclamation mark in the original remains and is followed by the three dots of the ellipsis.

> Days like this give sight a rest and allow other senses to function more freely. . . . It was either raining or pretending to rain or not raining at all, yet still appearing to rain in a sense that only certain old Northern dialects can either express verbally or not express, but *versionize,* as it were, through the ghost of a sound produced by a drizzle in a haze of grateful rose shrubs.
>
> —Vladimir Nabokov, *Transparent Things*

> What would Rossini have eaten late at night, when the sky was too bright with stars, too sculptural with cloud, too clever with nightingales, for him to go to bed, however pretty his companion or compliant nurse, what would he eat, while his kidneys ached and the moon sashayed across what he already knew must be one of the last lovely spring midnights of his life? . . . But what would he eat? Would he tinkle a bell, and a cadre of diligent, unsurprised servants fall into *sorbet* formation, or pull a mousse providently beforehand from the ferns around the ice-block in the double-doored chest? . . . just one more morsel of this after all adorable cosmos.
>
> —Robert Kelly, *A Line of Sight*

To punctuate the end of a quotation that is left deliberately incomplete as a sentence, three dots will suffice.

> Many of us remember the opening lines of *Lolita:* "Lolita, light of my life, fire of my loins. My sin, my soul. Lo-lee-ta: the tip of the tongue taking a trip of three steps . . ." But who has memorized other memorable passages from that book?